D1736162

Preface

Echoes of Life is a collection of short stories inspired by the multifaceted experiences of human existence in **INDIA** . Each story in this anthology captures a fragment of life, an echo that reverberates through the corridors of time, relationships, and self-discovery. The narratives are woven around themes of love, resilience, ambition, introspection, and the enduring human spirit, aiming to resonate with readers from all walks of life.

As I embarked on this literary journey, I found myself deeply moved by the simplicity of everyday events and the profound lessons they carry. These stories are not merely tales but reflections of emotions we often encounter—joys that warm our hearts, struggles that test our limits, and moments of revelation that reshape our understanding of life.

Through *Echoes of Life*, I have attempted to explore the subtleties of human behaviour and relationships, often drawing from observations and personal musings. The characters and settings, though **fictional**, are inspired by the diversity and richness of life around us, making them relatable and evocative.

This collection is an invitation to pause, reflect, and engage with the world through a lens of empathy and wonder. Each story, in its essence, seeks to remind us of the beauty and complexity of life, encouraging us to listen to the echoes that often go unnoticed in the humdrum of daily living.

I am deeply grateful to my family, friends, and readers whose encouragement has been the driving force behind this book. I hope *Echoes of Life* finds a place in your heart and offers a moment of solace, inspiration, or introspection.

Thank you for joining me on this journey of stories.

Prem Prakash Akhauri

akhauriprem@gmail.com

Contents

Story1

The sweetness of nostalgia

Prateek grew up in a sprawling industrial township nestled in a remote part of eastern India. His father, an engineer, was a respectable and humble man whose charismatic personality attracted everyone, from local politicians to small-town traders. As the youngest in the family, Prateek was adored by all. The township was home to two good schools, but a nearby Jesuit school stood out for its superior educational standards and holistic development approach.

The township's cosmopolitan environment, with employees from different parts of the country, fostered a culturally rich and inclusive community. Prateek and his older brother Rajesh were fortunate enough to study at the Jesuit school, while their younger siblings attended the local township school. The younger ones excelled in their studies, much to their father's delight, while Prateek and Rajesh managed only moderately good results.

When the Jesuit school announced a fee hike, their father warned the two brothers that if they didn't find a place in the top three of their class this year, they too would be transferred to the local school. Scared and embarrassed at the thought of losing face among their friends, the brothers decided to buckle down and prove their father wrong.

Prateek, though not the most studious, was bright and excelled in extracurricular activities. His popularity among teachers earned him the role of class monitor, a responsibility he juggled while shielding his mischievous classmates from the wrath of their strict teachers. His class was notorious for its pranksters, but their antics brought joy and laughter to everyone, including Prateek.

One day, during a moral science lesson, a Jesuit father visiting from New York joined their class. After introducing himself, he asked the students to open their books to a chapter titled Charity Begins at Home. Indra, the most mischievous boy in class, was asked to read aloud. True to his nature, Indra interspersed the reading with subtle abusive words, leaving the class stifling their laughter. The Jesuit father, though confused, maintained his composure.

"Boys," he said with a smile, "I enjoy your mirth, but a few words spoken need some improvement."After the class, the Jesuit father shared his observations with Mr. John, the school's registrar. Mr. John, quick to grasp what had happened, stormed into Prateek's classroom.

"Who's the monitor?" he bellowed.

Prateek stood up nervously. Mr. John demanded the names of the students who had read that day. Despite his innocence, Prateek's name was also noted. The group of boys was marched in front of the junior school and made to kneel while holding their ears, much to the amusement of the younger students watching through the windows. Later, they were issued memos to be signed by their parents.

Terrified of his father's reaction, Prateek met Mr. John privately and pleaded, "Sir, I didn't do anything! My father will pull me out of this school if he learns about this."After much persuasion, Mr. John exempted Prateek from punishment, but not without a stern warning.

As the annual exams approached, the pranks took a backseat, and everyone focused on their studies. However, fate had other plans. Their regular math teacher fell ill, and Mr. Das, an elderly substitute, was assigned to the class. Mr. Das, with his peculiar appearance and thick lenses, was a skilled teacher but suspicious of their notorious reputation."Revise the chapter on binomial theorem," he instructed, eyeing the class warily.

The boys, relieved at the prospect of a quiet class, relaxed—until a marble suddenly bounced across the floor and struck the blackboard.

"Who did that?" Mr. Das thundered. The class fell silent.

Turning to Prateek, he said, "You're the monitor. Write down the names of those not revising and indulging in pranks."

Caught between his role and loyalty to his friends, Prateek cleverly wrote down names—but instead of classmates, he listed popular Hindi movie stars. The boys, impressed by his quick thinking, whispered praises for his courage.

When the class ended, Mr. Das collected the names and marched Prateek to Mr. John's office. Sensing the impending disaster, several boys rushed to Mr. Das, pleading for Prateek's innocence.

"How can a monitor be so irresponsible?" Mr. Das fumed.

Indra, ever the dramatic one, sat on the floor and clutched Mr. Das's feet, begging for forgiveness. After much commotion, Prateek was let off with a warning, thanks to his classmates' intervention.

Decades later, the classmates reunited for a school reunion. As they reminisced, the harmless pranks and mischievous moments came alive once more. Prateek, now a successful and respectable man, couldn't help but laugh as they recounted the marble incident, Indra's antics, and the memo debacle.

"Those were the days," someone sighed. "If only we could relive them just once."

The group nodded in agreement, cherishing the bond and memories that had stood the test of time. Prateek smiled, realizing that it wasn't just the academics or achievements that had shaped him, but also the mischief, camaraderie, and life lessons learned in those formative years..**PPA**

Story 2.
Grandma and Bholu's Bond

The joyous cries of a newborn echoed through the village. A healthy, radiant baby boy had entered the world, spreading cheer in every corner of the family home. Everyone rejoiced, but no one was as thrilled as Lali, the mischievous elder sister, who ran to her grandmother with glee.

"Dadi, your Bholu has arrived!" she teased, her eyes sparkling with mischief.

Dadi, the matriarch of the family, was a woman of strong opinions and an even stronger personality. She looked at the baby in Lali's arms, noticing his striking features—sharp eyes, a perfectly shaped nose, and a robust frame. But her attention was drawn to his complexion, a deep shade of brown that reminded her of the monsoon soil.

Dadi frowned. "Lali, don't tease me. Look at him—his complexion has ruined the family's pride!"

Lali wasn't one to back down. She countered with her sharp wit. "Dadi, you always chant Krishna's name day and night. Look! He's just like Krishna! Mark my words, my Bholu will be as great as Him!"

Dadi waved her off. "Enough of your chatter, Lali. Go help your mother instead of pestering me!" she said, though a faint smile played on her lips.

As the years rolled by, little Bholu began to grow, and so did his charm. His playful antics brought the family endless joy, and his intelligence became the talk of the village. Yet, despite his achievements, Dadi remained aloof. Her heart seemed reserved for her eldest grandson from her step-son , Lalla, whom she adored.

"Bholu is too dark," Dadi often muttered under her breath, dismissing his accomplishments with a wave of her hand.

Lali, ever the loyal sister, stood firm by Bholu. "Dadi, you'll see. Bholu will do something no one in this family has ever done. He'll make you proud, even if you don't see it now!"

Bholu was too young to understand the subtle disdain, but as he grew older, he began to notice. He threw himself into his studies and worked harder than anyone else in the family. His sharp mind and determination soon earned him a scholarship to a prestigious college in the city.

When the news reached the village, it spread like wildfire. Everyone praised Dadi's lineage, crediting her blessings for Bholu's success. But Dadi remained unimpressed."Bholu may be smart, but Lalla is still the pride of this family," she insisted.

Years passed, and Bholu's hard work bore fruit. He became a respected businessman, building a name for himself in the city. He returned to the village with his achievements and a beautiful bride, hoping to earn the approval he had longed for since childhood.

Dadi's reaction, however, was as predictable as ever. "She's too modern," she whispered to the women of the family, eyeing Bholu's wife.

Despite her indifference, Bholu showered Dadi with affection and gifts. He renovated her room, bought her a comfortable chair, and even arranged for her favorite sweets to be delivered regularly. Yet, no matter what he did, Dadi's affection remained elusive.

One day, Lali confronted Dadi. "Dadi, why are you so stubborn? Can't you see how much Bholu loves you? He's done everything to make you happy!"

Dadi sighed, her eyes softening for a moment. "Lali, you don't understand. My heart has always been tied to Lalla. It's not about dislike. It's just the way things are."

Time, however, doesn't wait for anyone. Dadi's health began to decline, and she spent most of her days resting in her favorite chair. She often called out for Lalla, her voice weak but insistent. Bholu, though quietly heartbroken, stayed by her side, attending to her every need.

When Dadi's final moment came, it was Bholu who performed her last rites with dignity and grace. Tears streamed down his face as he bid farewell to the woman who had been both his critic and his guide.

In the days that followed, Bholu often sat in Dadi's empty room, lost in thought. He remembered her scolding, her sharp tongue, but also the hidden care she had shown in her own way.

"Dadi," he whispered one evening, his voice thick with emotion, "your Bholu still remembers you. I hope, wherever you are, you're finally proud of me."..**PPA**

Story 3.

Naveen's nostalgic sojourn: Between two worlds

Naveen often found himself drifting back to the simple joys of his younger days. Mornings in those times began with a steaming cup of tea, richly infused with cinnamon, ginger, and cardamom. The aroma was enough to awaken the senses, but it was the ritual of reading the newspaper that truly anchored his mornings. Sports pages were always the first stop, followed by the editorial section—an unspoken rule passed down by his father—and finally the headlines of the front page. Often, one cup of tea wasn't enough, and the session extended to two, sometimes three, cups, as winter sunshine bathed the garden in a soft glow.

His first stroll of the day, a casual walk through the garden, felt like an unconscious connection with nature. The neighbor's occasional request for a shared tea session was a heartwarming moment, one that added a special charm to those mornings. Then came the visit to the local "chaupal"—a modest tea stall that doubled as the village's debating ground. Here, world affairs were dissected with fervor, every discussion punctuated with laughter, arguments, and a few persistent dissidents.

Those days were filled with warmth, community, and a rhythm that felt timeless.

But time, as it often does, brought change. Naveen's journey from his idyllic hometown to a bustling mega-city for a job was fraught with heartache. The looming thought of leaving behind the simplicity of home and the people he cherished cast a shadow over his new beginning. The city's relentless pace soon engulfed him. The race to make ends meet consumed his peace—children's education, mounting medical expenses, and the ever-rising cost of living left little room for reflection or joy.

Years flew by. Grey hairs gave way to white, and wrinkles began to map the passage of time on his face. One day, the opportunity arose to revisit the place he had left so long ago. With a mixture of excitement and trepidation, Naveen returned to his hometown. He found his friends, almost untouched by time, still devoted to their familiar routines. The "chaupal" was the same, with its animated discussions and comforting camaraderie. Yet, Naveen felt like an outsider in the very place that once defined him.

His friends seemed content, their lives buoyed by the simplicity of rural living and government provisions. Naveen, however, was restless. The anxieties of his city life clung to him, and the looming pile of unfinished work in his apartment left him uneasy. He had climbed the corporate ladder, but the pressures of high taxes and an unrelenting cost of living weighed him down.

Now, with his working years behind him, Naveen faced an inner conflict. Where should he settle? Could he return to the calm of his hometown, or had the city's demands shaped him into someone too restless to embrace that peace? He tried, time and again, to adapt to his old life, but the allure of solitude and the illusion of satisfaction he had built in the city held him captive.

Naveen's story is a reflection of so many lives—a tale of displacement, adaptation, and the quiet longing for simpler times. Life, driven by circumstances, moves forward relentlessly, leaving us to grapple with the choices we've made and the roads we've taken. As Naveen often thought to himself, "Perhaps the answer lies not in choosing between two worlds, but in finding peace within."..**PPA**

Story 4.

The Weave of Fate

Raj's birth was a moment of joy for the bustling Nath family. The village celebrated with drums, sweets, and prayers, considering his arrival auspicious. Nath,

Raj's father, a staunch believer in astrology, summoned the family astrologer and a pandit. After hours of deliberation, they proclaimed that Raj was destined for greatness. The family's hope soared; they believed he was the one who would restore their dwindling pride.

The Nath household was a joint family of 28 members, led by the matriarch Rukmini. She was a woman forged in adversity, raising her five children after her husband's untimely death. Her husband, an eccentric lover of the *Ramayana* and compulsive eater, had passed away unexpectedly, leaving her to navigate poverty and social challenges with unwavering resolve.

Her younger brother Dashrat, orphaned like her, had accompanied her into her marital home as a child. Rukmini raised him alongside her children, especially Raj, who became Dashrat's closest companion. While Rukmini's husband had passed on his fatalistic beliefs to Raj, she tried to instill in her children the importance of hard work and karma.

Raj excelled in school, thanks to Dashrat, who ferried him to the middle school seven kilometers away on a rusty old bicycle gifted by the village pradhan. Dashrat was a matriculate but intelligent, with a knack for connecting with people. He juggled multiple responsibilities, ensuring Raj could focus on his studies. Raj's academic brilliance and his football skills made him a local hero, and Dashrat's pride in him was boundless.

While Raj thrived in school, Dashrat sought ways to improve his own life. He earned the trust of a local shopkeeper, eventually managing his stores. It was during this time that Dashrat met Rupa, the shopkeeper's daughter. Their love blossomed despite societal barriers, but caste differences and her father's conservative outlook cast a shadow over their relationship.

Rupa urged Dashrat to elope, but he stood firm, believing in a legitimate union. Tragedy struck when her father passed away suddenly. The village, wary of caste issues, debated their union. With support from Rukmini and the sarpanch's son, Dashrat and Rupa fled to a nearby town and married in a quiet ceremony. The couple's resilience earned them eventual acceptance in their community.

Meanwhile, Raj continued to shine, inspired by Dashrat's sacrifices and Rukmini's wisdom. He embodied the family's hopes, proving that grit and determination could transform fate. His success became a beacon for the next generation.

Years later, Rukmini, now frail but wise, reflected on the journey of her family. "Life begins in fate's cradle," she often said, "but it's our choices that define the tapestry we leave behind." Through trials and tribulations, love and resilience, the family had not only survived but thrived, leaving a legacy of courage and hope for generations to come..**PPA**

Story 5.

Lakshmi's tale of strength and resilience

Lakshmi was the eldest daughter of a humble village teacher, who, with six daughters, was burdened with the task of arranging their marriages within his modest means. As the years passed, his worry grew, especially for Lakshmi, whose marriage he believed would ease some of the family's challenges. Lakshmi, with her astonishing beauty, fair complexion, and graceful demeanor, drew admiration from everyone in the village.

Finally, her father found a match for her— Biswa, a widower with a son and a daughter. Biswa worked as a clerk in the local sarpanch's office, earning enough to sustain his family. He also supplemented his income by writing letters for the illiterate villagers. A devout man, Biswa was known for his daily recitations of the Ramayana and his compassionate nature.

After their marriage, Biswa became captivated by Lakshmi's beauty and her ability to manage the household and his children skillfully. Despite his modest income, he never turned away anyone seeking help, often telling Lakshmi, "God repays you in abundance for kindness extended." His devotion and humility earned him the respect of the entire village, who began to revere him as a pious man, especially after he claimed to have had a vision of Lord Ram.

Life moved forward, and Lakshmi and Biswa had two more children, making it a family of six. Despite their limited means, Lakshmi ensured her children excelled in school, often urging them to study and guiding them as best she could, even though she herself was illiterate. Her encouragement and discipline bore fruit, as all four children thrived academically.

However, their happiness was short-lived. On the morning of Ramnavmi, Biswa passed away unexpectedly. His eldest son, Narayan, broke the tragic news to the family, plunging Lakshmi into grief. Yet, amidst her sorrow, she resolved to stand strong for her children.

Lakshmi approached the school master, who held Biswa in high regard, and he assured her that Narayan would receive a government school job on compassionate grounds. Lakshmi persevered, managing the family with determination and encouraged Lakshman to resume his education, promising that the family's situation would soon improve. With scholarships for her younger children and her tireless efforts, the family gradually found stability.

Years passed, and Lakshmi's hard work paid off. All four of her children secured respectable jobs, earning admiration in the community. Her father, who had struggled for years to marry off her younger sisters, found peace as they all settled into happy lives. Lakshmi took care of her ailing father in his final years, fulfilling her duty as a devoted daughter..**PPA**

Story 6.

Sohan's life

Sohan and Rafiq were very good friends who spent most of their days pursuing activities other than studies. Sohan was the eldest son of Nath, who had migrated from a sleepy town in eastern India to Delhi to work for a multinational company. Since Nath grew up in a joint family, he left his children, Sohan and Rakhi, in his hometown Bangdar under the care of his elder brother. He believed that growing up in a large family setup would instill values and confidence in his children, contrasting with the isolated nuclear family life in Delhi. Nath felt that children thrived in the secure and nurturing environment of a joint family. Moreover, Bangdar had an excellent high school where Nath himself had completed his matriculation before moving to Delhi for his Graduation and degree in Law.

Nath's elder brother was a kind and indulgent man who pampered Sohan, ensuring he felt no resentment toward his upbringing. However, this leniency allowed Sohan to live unchecked. He had plenty of time and freedom to engage in pranks, fights, and displays of dominance, which bolstered his pride. A handsome boy with a sharp intellect, Rohan lacked proper guidance. Even the school teachers, who often praised his intelligence and leadership qualities, were unaware of his frequent misadventures and class-skipping with his quiet friend, Rafiq.

As the festival of Holi approached, Sohan and his friends began their yearly preparations for the grandest "Holika Dahan" celebration, a Hindu festival marking the triumph of good over evil. They collected wood and twigs to create an enormous pyre. However, a rivalry with Shyam and his friends, who were also building a large pile, soon escalated. To outdo Shyam, Sohan resorted to borrowing, begging, or even stealing materials. Those who resisted often found their wood missing the next morning. Complaints to Nath's brother went unheard, as he believed Rohan was working hard for a noble cause.

The night before Holika Dahan, Sohan and his friends planned to raid Shyam's pile, which was heavily guarded. A fierce fight broke out, but Rohan emerged victorious, seizing half of Shyam's pile and adding it to his own. That night, the Holika Dahan celebration in Rohan's neighborhood was a grand success, solidifying his image as a dominant protector of the area. During the festivities, Rohan noticed Radha, beautifully dressed and radiating charm. Overwhelmed by romantic feelings, he joined the dance and stood close to her. That night left an indelible mark on his heart.

Sohan, however, had hardly studied for his annual exams and grew anxious about his father discovering his activities. Failing to meet his father's expectations might result in being summoned to Delhi, a prospect he dreaded, especially after his newfound infatuation with Radha. Nonetheless, Sohan managed to pass with 72% marks, which was enough to keep his family hopeful about his future.

One day, while fishing at a nearby pond, Sohan confided his feelings for Radha to Rafiq. Shocked, Rafiq reminded him that Radha's engagement had been performed years earlier, and her father was planning her marriage that summer. Devastated, Sohan turned to alcohol and smoking to cope with his heartbreak. For weeks, he seemed withdrawn and lifeless, contemplating meeting Radha but refraining to preserve his reputation in the neighborhood. He resolved to move on, though the pain of unrequited love lingered.

That summer, Nath and his wife visited Bangdar with their two younger children, relishing the local mangoes, rohu fish, and occasional drinks with his elder brother. While Nath enjoyed the familial warmth, Sohan remained restless. One evening, Shyam and his friends launched a surprise attack on Sohan and Rafiq over their old rivalry. Unprepared, the two were brutally beaten and ended up in the hospital. Sohan required stitches, and Rafiq suffered a hairline fracture. Furious and alarmed, Nath confronted Sohan about his vagabond lifestyle and declared, "Get ready to leave for Delhi with us." Unable to resist his father's commanding tone, Sohan reluctantly complied.

Back in Delhi, Sohan completed his graduation and enrolled in law school under Nath's vigilant supervision. Nostalgia often swept over him as he reminisced about his days in Bangdar, his friendship with Rafiq, and his memories of Radha. Leveraging his innate intelligence and oratory skills, Sohan excelled in law school and eventually joined his father's law firm, carving a promising path for his future..**PPA**

Story7

Raghu's travel from skepticism to faith

Raghu was born into a middle-class family consisting of his father and three siblings. From a young age, he witnessed his mother struggling with poor health, which consumed a significant portion of the family's budget. His father, an accountant in a private financial company, worked tirelessly to provide a comfortable life and ensure that his children received a good education.

His parents were deeply religious and believed firmly in the idea that God would take care of everything. The temple priest, Panditji, was a regular visitor to their home, often engaging the family in various rituals and practices. Growing up, Raghu absorbed these traditions, believing that their religious devotion might bring some good fortune to the family.

However, tragedy struck when Raghu lost his mother to her illness. His father, overwhelmed with grief, slipped into depression, skipping work and facing the threat of suspension due to repeated absenteeism. At this critical juncture, Raghu, a bright and responsible boy, stepped up to support the family. He started tutoring young students, earning just enough to cover his education and household expenses.

During his teenage years, Raghu would often sit under the shade of mango trees after school, reflecting on life and its uncertainties. Panditji's recent sermon on the Bhagavad Gita left a mark on him, particularly the emphasis on karma—the belief that good actions yield good results. This philosophy deeply resonated with Raghu, instilling in him a firm belief in hard work and the rewards it brings.

As Raghu contemplated life, he began to develop a unique perspective. He reasoned that divinity lay in what one could see and experience through their senses. To him, his parents, who had brought him into this world, were no less than gods, and nature itself was a divine entity deserving of respect and preservation. He coined his own idea of "Nature God," advocating for its reverence and protection.

Raghu often debated Panditji about metaphysical concepts. The priest would try to convince him with analogies like, "You don't see air, but can you deny its existence and importance for survival?" While Raghu acknowledged the wisdom in Panditji's words, his belief system remained rooted in tangible realities, leaning toward an agnostic worldview.

Raghu's dedication to his studies paid off. He earned a PhD in environmental science and cleared the prestigious Indian Forest Services examination, fulfilling his dream of living close to nature. He married Radha, a sociology PhD who skillfully balanced her family responsibilities with her academic pursuits. Together, they built a harmonious life.

Raghu's father, now elderly, agreed to move in with the couple. They settled in a picturesque town in Uttarakhand, surrounded by natural beauty and fresh mountain air. This new environment, coupled with the warmth of a happy family, restored his father's health. Raghu also facilitated the marriage of his third sister through a traditional gotra arrangement, further solidifying family ties.

Raghu's professional journey flourished. He earned a reputation for his strong stance against poaching and the illegal smuggling of precious wood. Despite receiving threats from politicians and criminals, Raghu remained undeterred, thanks to the unwavering support of his team and superiors. His efforts earned him accolades and national recognition, and he was invited to speak at prominent conferences worldwide.

Life seemed perfect until tragedy struck again. Raghu's young son fell gravely ill, and his condition deteriorated with each passing day. Despite consulting the best doctors across the country, no one could diagnose the cause of his illness. Radha, devastated by the situation, began to show signs of physical and emotional strain.

One evening, Raghu's father, ever the believer, said to him, "Don't worry, son. God has His own way of testing us. Have faith, and everything will be fine."

The next morning, on his way to work, Raghu stopped at a red light. A sadhu appeared seemingly out of nowhere and said, "You look troubled, son. Have faith; God will heal all your troubles soon." Before Raghu could respond, the sadhu disappeared. Raghu looked around, but the mysterious figure was nowhere to be seen.

Miraculously, within a week, his son began to recover. To the astonishment of the doctors, the boy was completely healthy within a month.

This experience left Raghu deeply introspective. He replayed the sadhu's words in his mind and began to question his long-held beliefs. For the first time, he considered the possibility of a higher power—one beyond human comprehension, capable of creation, preservation, and destruction.

Moved by this newfound understanding, Raghu and Radha visited the local temple together. They bowed their heads and folded their hands in prayer, offering gratitude to the divine force that had guided them through their trials...**PPA**

Story 8

The Life of Dr. Suresh

"Dr. Sahab has arrived! Please inform Giri Babu," the peon shouted as Dr. Suresh alighted from his ambassador car. The driver respectfully opened the gate for him as he walked majestically toward his cabin. Giri Babu, his trusted assistant, quickly briefed him about the day's schedule, including meetings, surgeries, and the OPD lineup.

Dr. Suresh, the Civil Surgeon of Indri district in Bihar, was a revered figure. The people of Indri had unwavering faith in his skills and rarely considered going to big city hospitals. His morning began with a round of the hospital wards, where patients eagerly awaited his examination and further instructions. For them, "Doctor Sahab" was more than a surgeon; he was a lifeline.

Later that day, the local Member of Parliament, infamous for his criminal background, called Dr. Suresh to request treatment for two henchmen injured in a police encounter. Despite the ethical dilemma, Dr. Suresh treated them with the same commitment, earning the MP's gratitude.After a long and demanding day, Dr. Suresh returned home. Following a brief interaction with his family, he headed to the club, where he enjoyed a game of bridge and his favorite whiskey. Elections for the state legislature were approaching, and the local MLA frequently sought his advice, valuing Dr. Suresh's influence and standing in the community.

At home, his routine included a refreshing bath followed by reciting the *Hanuman Chalisa*. Observing wrinkles near his wife Devi's neck, he said, "I'll get you a cream tomorrow. Apply it twice daily." The couple's mornings began at 5 a.m. with tea and a walk in their garden. Dr. Suresh found joy curating their sprawling lawn, feeding rabbits, and caring for their cow and buffalo, tasks managed with the help of Lalu and Bhagat, who lived in the servant quarters. Devi nurtured her exclusive vegetable garden, a skill she had inherited from her landlord father.

Dr. Suresh's journey was remarkable. A prodigious child with an eidetic memory, he excelled academically, earning a gold medal in his Master of Surgery from a premier medical college. Initially setting up a practice in his hometown Madhpur, he quickly gained wealth and respect. His loyal compounder, Bhawani, often managed the clinic in his absence.

During a medical conference, Dr. Suresh learned about a vacancy in the Railways. His father encouraged him to apply, emphasizing the prestige, discipline, and balance the job offered. He secured the position, posted near Nainital, where he thrived and became a respected independent head at Izzatnagar. Despite the success, his longing to serve his home state persisted.

Devi supported his decision to return, provided their children received quality education. At Indri, Dr. Suresh transformed the hospital with modern equipment and efficient practices. He became a beloved figure, attending community events and religious sermons. A chance meeting with his distant cousin, Guru Ramdas, deepened his spiritual inclinations.

Dr. Suresh's efforts to combat corruption at the hospital earned him respect but also strained his health. As his sons established themselves and his daughters married, he decided to return to Madhpur. Devi, equally excited, shared his enthusiasm for their new chapter.

Residents of Indri gathered in large numbers to bid him an emotional farewell. As the train departed, Dr. Suresh felt a mix of sadness for leaving Indri and joy for returning home. Nearing retirement, he settled comfortably in Madhpur, treating poor patients for free and finding solace in spirituality. His days were filled with peace, contentment, and the wisdom gleaned from reading scriptures.

Dr. Suresh's life was a testament to dedication, humility, and the pursuit of service above self..**PPA**

Story 9

The Carefree Philosopher: Lalan's way of life

Lalan's mornings always began with an air of calm and ease, unlike the frenzy that seemed to engulf the rest of the world. People rushed to fulfill their responsibilities, chasing their desires, but Lalan's unhurried pace never changed. His philosophy was simple and consistent: "The provider is one Ram, and the rest of the world are mere beggars."

As he lounged on his charpoy outside the tea stall, sipping his usual cup of tea, his mother's voice echoed from inside their modest home: "You good-for-nothing! What will become of you after I'm gone? At least think about your future!"

Lalan, unperturbed, chuckled and muttered to himself, "The future is in the hands of the one above. Why worry?"

At the tea stall, someone nearby was singing a soulful tune: "What did I gain? What did I lose?" The words resonated with Lalan, who found himself reflecting on the simplicity of his life. After a brief nap under the shade of the banyan tree, he awoke feeling refreshed, just as a minor accident narrowly missed occurring on the busy road.

"Jako rakhe saiyan, maar sake na koi,"-
"The one protected by almighty cannot be harmed"; someone remarked, referring to the divine protection. Lalan smiled, deep in thought. "Life is indeed strange," he mused. "People worry endlessly, but isn't it the divine above who writes our destiny?"

As the day wound down, Lalan strolled to the local hangout spot where his friends had gathered. They were engrossed in discussing the grandeur of their cars and their rising social status. When Lalan arrived, they teased him: "Why don't you earn some money, Lalan? Buy a car and we'll throw a party!"

Lalan laughed and replied, "Why burden myself with loans and EMIs? Life is a journey, and there are plenty of ways to travel. I'm content with what I have. "

His friends burst out laughing, calling him "the carefree philosopher." One of them quipped, "You should work on your fitness, Lalan . Look at you! How will you manage life with that flabby body?"

Lalan, still smiling, retorted, "Strength doesn't come from muscles alone. True power lies in the strength of the mind. Look at history—great warriors had both physical strength and unshakeable resolve."

Another friend, more curious than teasing, asked, "Don't you ever worry about anything?"

Lalan leaned back, his grin widening. "What's there to worry about? What's gone is gone. Tomorrow will come in its own way, and whatever happens, I'll face it just like today."

His friends laughed, one of them pointing out, "With this attitude, who's going to marry you?"

Lalan shrugged. "Relationships exist in many forms. But tying myself down in a bond that doesn't suit me? That's not for me."

The teasing turned serious as one of them remarked, "You'll be left behind in life's race."

Lalal 's response was calm and steady: "Those who run too fast often trip and fall. Life isn't about racing; it's about walking with a clear mind and enjoying the journey. Slow and steady wins not just the race, but life itself."

Finally, one friend couldn't hold back and asked bluntly, "What's your identity, Lalan? What makes you special?"

Lalan's eyes sparkled with contentment. "I am happy," he said simply. "I entertain people, stay connected with nature, spend time on my fields, sing songs, and live a simple, peaceful life. Isn't that enough?"

The group fell silent, taken aback by Lalan's clarity and conviction. In their pursuit of material wealth and status, they realized they had overlooked the profound joy of simplicity and peace.

Lalan, the carefree philosopher, had once again left his mark. He may not have run in the same race as his friends, but his drumbeat of life played a melody that no one could resist tapping their feet to.

One friend witted , "Lalan's philosophy reminds us that happiness isn't about running faster or accumulating more; it's about finding peace in simplicity and walking at your own pace, in tune with life's rhythm"..**PPA**

Story 10
Dhanna and the Nifty Dance

Dhanna was a simple man with a big dream: to get rich quick. One day, a self-proclaimed financial guru told him, "If you want to make money, you must learn the Nifty dance."

Dhanna scratched his head. "What kind of dance is this that makes money?"

The guru's eager disciple chimed in, "Sir, right now an 'Inverted Hammer' is forming on the charts. Soon, Nifty will skyrocket!"

Confused but intrigued, Dhanna set out to understand this mysterious Nifty dance. On his way home, he ran into a dance master. Dhanna thought, "This must be fate!"

"Sir," Dhanna asked with utmost seriousness, "I've heard of Tandav, Disco, and Classical dances, but what is this Nifty dance?"

The dance master, brimming with pride, began rattling off a list of Indian classical dances. "There's Bharatanatyam, Kathak, Odissi, Kathakali, Kuchipudi, Manipuri, Mohiniyattam, and Sattriya," he said.

Dhanna's eyes glazed over, and he nodded along, pretending to understand.

But Dhanna's goal was money, not culture. So he decided to dive into the world of stocks and became utterly engrossed in the so-called "Nifty dance." Trusting the disciple's confident assurances, Dhanna poured his entire savings into Nifty.

What happened next was nothing short of a chaotic Tandav. The Nifty index seemed to have a mind of its own.One moment, it leaped up like a Bharatanatyam performer hitting a high note. The next, it tumbled down like a clumsy student attempting Kuchipudi for the first time. Sometimes it stayed eerily still, like a dancer waiting for the cue, and other times it spun wildly, leaving Dhanna's head spinning faster than the stock market charts.

"Patience, my friend," the financial guru reassured him. "This is just a phase. Nifty will stabilize, and you'll make big bucks. Keep investing more!"Dhanna, a believer now, emptied his pockets and waited for his fortune to arrive.

Dhanna's savings were all but gone, and his dreams of wealth had taken a nosedive. Every day, he watched the financial news channels, performing Anulom-Vilom breathing exercises to calm his nerves. He even started chanting prayers, hoping for a miracle to recover his lost money.

But life had other plans. With no savings left, Dhanna decided to put his newfound interest in dance to practical use. He enrolled in a Bharatanatyam class, mastered the basics, and began teaching children in his neighborhood.

Every evening, after his classes, Dhanna would still glance at the stock market ticker. Watching Nifty's erratic "dance" reminded him of his own missteps. Sighing deeply, he'd collapse onto his bed, mumbling, "If only I'd learned the real dance instead of chasing dreams in the market!"

Sometimes, life teaches you the real dance.Well, he's now a master of Bharatanatyam and an expert storyteller of how he once danced with Nifty and fell flat on his face!..**PPA**

Story 11

Sudesh's life of despair to triumph

Sudesh sat quietly, reminiscing about the day that had shaped his life. It had been one of countless struggles, and he felt like everything had been sacrificed at the altar of the medical entrance examination—a pursuit that had turned into an endless cycle of hope and disappointment. Time and again, he confided in his closest friend, Raju, saying, "Either I become a doctor, or I do nothing else in life."

Sudesh's father, a highly respected doctor, had dreamed of passing the mantle to his son. Sudesh, a bright student, shared the same aspiration but was haunted by repeated failures. Raju, in his usual comforting manner, would remind him, "Life is an arduous journey, my friend, and time is the best healer. Once you move past this phase, I'm certain the fighter in you will set things right."

But Sudesh's despondency ran deep. "Whenever an ambulance with its red siren passes by," he once told Raju, "I freeze in place, thinking it's all over for me. A heavy cloud of despair engulfs me."

What Raju didn't know was that Sudesh had quietly applied for a bank entrance examination as a backup. The results were expected soon. That day, when his mother handed him a registered post from the PSEB, his heart raced. He knew they didn't send rejection letters. Clutching the envelope, he felt his hands tremble. Unable to summon the courage to open it, he grabbed his bicycle and pedaled to Raju's house.

On the way, Sudesh contemplated taking a detour to Namrata's house. Namrata, a bright and accomplished medical student who had cleared the entrance exam the previous year, was someone Sudesh admired deeply. But Namrata's father, ever suspicious of Sudesh's intentions, was watering the garden. He had made no secret of his disapproval of Sudesh, convinced he was a "good-for-nothing" who wasn't worthy of his daughter. Defeated by circumstance, Sudesh turned away and continued toward Raju's house.

Back home, Sudesh's father was fuming. He had discovered Sudesh's alternate plans and was deeply disappointed. "You mustn't give up hope so easily," he said sternly. "I'm confident you can be an excellent doctor. This failure is just a small hurdle. Dr. Raman, the renowned surgeon, is opening a medical college in our town with support from the local MLA. I've hinted at contributing to the college if he ensures a seat for you. By the time you graduate, the college will surely gain government recognition. This is your chance."

Sudesh listened quietly but felt uneasy. He didn't want to succeed through favors. His determination was to become a doctor on his own merit. He slipped out of the house to visit Namrata, seeking clarity.

"Sudesh," Namrata said gently, "I've always thought of you as a better student than me. I don't know why God has put you through this, but I believe your father knows what's best for you. You should trust his wisdom."Her next words lit a spark in Sudesh's heart. "And after you graduate, we can open a clinic together—and, with our parents' blessings, consider starting a life together."

Namrata's words gave Sudesh the strength he needed. He poured his heart and soul into his medical studies. With time, he not only excelled but also became the topper of his batch. During practical sessions, his professors praised his precise hands during dissections, marking him as a natural-born surgeon.

But as the MS entrance exams approached, Sudesh's old fears resurfaced. The memory of past failures haunted him. Namrata, now pursuing her MS, stood by him, offering valuable tips to tackle multiple-choice questions, his Achilles' heel. With her guidance, Sudesh cleared the exam with a high rank, earning a coveted seat in MS.

During this time, tragedy struck Namrata's family. Her father suffered a fatal heart attack, leaving her devastated. But his parting words—urging her to become the best doctor in town—echoed in her mind, driving her forward. A year after her father's demise, she completed her MS and prepared to enter the professional world.

Sudesh, meanwhile, had matured into a confident and accomplished medical student. His father, who had once been so frustrated with Sudesh's failures, now watched with pride as his son thrived. Even Namrata's father, before his passing, had softened toward Sudesh, acknowledging his potential.

That summer, with the blessings of both families, Sudesh and Namrata tied the knot in a beautiful ceremony.After completing their MS degrees, Sudesh and Namrata decided to move to a nearby city to start their own clinic. Their dedication to their profession, combined with their compassionate approach, quickly earned them a stellar reputation. They became known not only for their medical expertise but also for their commitment to providing free services to the poor and destitute.

Sudesh often reflected on his journey— from despair and doubt to love and triumph. The lessons he learned along the way shaped him into not just a successful doctor, but a better human being. Together, he and Namrata built a legacy of healing and hope, fulfilling their dreams and those of their families..**PPA**

Story 12

A tale of life lessons and second chances

Life's journey takes you through unexpected paths, and for Rahul and Mahesh, their new chapter as trainees in a leading pharmaceutical company was no exception. Having recently qualified for the prestigious training program, the two young men quickly bonded and decided to share a room during their training period.

Mahesh, with an air of excitement, shared, "Rahul, this was my first time travelling in a second AC compartment. The entire journey, I couldn't stop thinking about the fantastic pay and perks this job shall offer. I almost wished the train ride never ended."

Rahul laughed and replied, "You're lucky your journey was short. My trip to Mohali from Hyderabad was much longer, but I enjoyed every bit of it. It's quite a leap from the non-AC second-class rides we took for the entrance exams in Jaipur, isn't it?"

Both of them marveled at how quickly life had changed. The discussion soon turned to their training schedule, which included a five-day outbound session in Manali. Mahesh, grinning mischievously, remarked, "I see plenty of girls in our batch. This training is going to be fun!"

Coming from a small town in eastern India, Mahesh had spent years under the watchful eyes of his parents, being the eldest son with three unmarried sisters. Talking to girls was seen as a transgression where he came from, but now he saw a whole new world opening up.

The training center, as per their reckoning, was nothing short of a five-star facility, complete with air-conditioned rooms, tea and coffee makers, geysers, free Wi-Fi, and TVs. The gymnasium and sports center were state-of-the-art. After settling in, they indulged in a lavish multi-cuisine buffet dinner before strolling through the serene campus.

The next morning, eager to make a good impression, they attended their induction classes. However, as the sessions dragged on, their curiosity about their batchmates, particularly the female ones, began to distract them. By the third day, boredom set in, and a brave trainee slipped out to the cafeteria. Rahul and Mahesh, unable to resist, soon joined the exodus, forming a gang of nine to ten regular absentees.

Their antics did not go unnoticed. Mr. Bhupinder Singh, the training Head, had spies stationed throughout the campus. The list of absconders quickly reached his desk. The next morning, the culprits were summoned to his office, where they were admonished for breaking discipline. "Your training period might be extended," he warned, "and that means staying on a stipend instead of regular pay."

Suitably chastened, the trainees filled the classroom the next day. But restless as ever, Rahul and Mahesh found ways to sneak out for their periodic smoking breaks, a strict no-no on campus. They even managed to bribe the campus spy, ensuring their escapades went unnoticed.

Despite their mischief, the looming qualifying examination brought a sense of urgency. Mahesh, under pressure to secure a regular position to support his family, sought hints about the exam from Mr. Bhupinder Singh, leveraging his knack for "jugaad" (resourceful problem-solving). Both Rahul and Mahesh passed, joining the 100% pass rate as the company hurried to deploy trainees for a massive production order.

Elated by their success, the duo decided to celebrate with a trip to Kasol, a picturesque spot known for its adventurous allure. "Let's leave early tomorrow," Mahesh said, "before Mr. Bhupinder catches wind of our plan." With the campus spy's help, they slipped out and boarded the first bus to Kasol.

Mahesh wished Radhika, a fellow trainee from Rampur, would join them, but she declined, wary of the place's reputation. The boys, however, immersed themselves in the escapade, indulging in Kasol's offerings. After a day of wandering, they fell asleep in a park, only to be woken by the evening chill. They checked into a nearby inn, exhausted but thrilled by their adventure.

Back at the campus, Mr. Singh grew concerned when the two didn't show up. When calls to their phones went unanswered, he informed their parents, who arrived in a state of panic. Mr. Singh also alerted Mr. Sahu, the director, who calmed the situation. "There's no need to involve the police yet," he said. "Their belongings are still in their room, and I've contacted the local police in Kasol to look for them."

By evening, the Kasol police returned the boys to the campus. Disheveled and visibly embarrassed, they faced a stern confrontation with their parents, Mr. Singh, and Mr. Sahu.

Mr. Sahu addressed them calmly but firmly. "Look, boys, we all have desires to indulge in activities without considering the consequences. But as professionals, you must discipline yourselves and conduct with dignity. Your actions deserve termination, but I will give you one chance to prove your commitment. The company sees great potential in you, and your families have high hopes. Do not let them down."

He concluded with a directive: "Attend the session on 'Managing Self and Others' once more. It will help you reflect on your actions."

The reprimand was a wake-up call. Both Rahul and Mahesh apologized sincerely, vowing to focus on their careers. Mahesh, glancing at Radhika, noticed a flicker of approval and hope in her eyes—a silent encouragement to rise above his mistakes.

From that day onward, the duo dedicated themselves to their roles, proving their worth and earning respect. The experience became a defining moment in their journey, shaping them into professionals who understood the value of discipline and responsibility.Life offers second chances, but it is up to us to seize them and rise above our past mistakes..**PPA**

Story 13

Randhir's struggle between love, and hope

Randhir was a teenager, deeply dissatisfied with his life. The nearby school teacher often urged him to enroll in school, but his words felt like careless remarks to Randhir. He was painfully aware of his family's financial struggles, and no one had ever extended a helping hand to secure free education for him. Instead, he spent his days playing *gulli danda* and *kancha* with his friend Bharat, who would occasionally teach him bits of language and life lessons.

Randhir, however, was not one to settle. Gifted with good health and keen observation, he dreamed of a better life—one where he could earn a decent living and support his family. One day, he spoke to his father about moving to a nearby city for work. "With Goddess Saraswati's blessings," he said, "I might even find a way to study." His father, struggling with destitution, saw this as an opportunity for some relief and gave his hesitant approval.

Randhir's elder brother, a wayward drifter, had long severed ties with the family. Randhir barely had a relationship with him and saw no point in sharing his plans. Determined, he set off the next morning, boarding a crowded general compartment train bound for the city. Bharat escorted him to the station and, with a pat on his shoulder, said, "One day, you'll return as a rich man."

Bharat's uncle, who worked as a security supervisor at a construction site, had assured him of a job for Randhir as a security guard. After a gruelling 15-hour journey, cramped in a tiny seat, Randhir arrived at the construction site. Bharat's uncle welcomed him warmly, showing him to the labour camp and arranging for him to meet the site manager.

The manager was impressed by Randhir's physique and alertness. "You'll earn Rs. 15,000 a month," he explained, "plus extra for overtime. We also offer group insurance, provident fund, and health coverage." Though Randhir didn't fully understand the details, he knew he had a chance to earn enough for his family. That evening,

Bharat's uncle invited him to dinner, where Randhir met Jaya, Bharat's cousin.

Jaya was a charming, resilient young woman who had lost her mother the previous year. Her father, now solely responsible for her future, was already planning her marriage before embarking on a pilgrimage. Randhir was struck by her beauty and strength, and thoughts of her lingered in his mind as he settled into his new life at the camp.

The labor camp was lively, with workers from different parts of the country singing folk songs and cooking together. Randhir quickly adapted to his new job and impressed the manager with his vigilance. "We've had thefts at night," the manager said. "If you take the night shift, you'll earn an extra allowance." Randhir eagerly agreed, knowing every rupee mattered.

On Sundays, Randhir ventured into the city, where he befriended a mall security guard named Raju. Raju shared stories of his job and encouraged Randhir to switch to mall security, which offered better pay and a safer environment. Randhir, however, remained focused on saving as much as possible.

One day, tragedy struck. Jaya's father was diagnosed with liver cirrhosis due to excessive drinking and passed away shortly after. Jaya, devastated and alone, received a small compensation amount but was unsure of her future. Randhir, moved by her plight, decided to propose marriage.

Jaya agreed to marry Randhir, and they soon moved into a small rented space in an unauthorized colony near the mall. With Jaya's compensation money, they bought a sewing machine, and she began stitching clothes—a skill her mother had taught her. Meanwhile, Randhir secured a better-paying job at the mall, often working double shifts to support their growing family.

Life slowly improved. Randhir and Jaya welcomed two sons and were determined to give them a better life. Their modest home now had essential amenities like a fridge, TV, toys for the kids, and even an air cooler. The boys were enrolled in a good local school, and Randhir worked tirelessly to meet the rising expenses.

After nearly a decade, Randhir decided to visit his village with his family. His parents were happy to see him and appreciated the financial support he had been sending over the years. Randhir immediately went to meet Bharat, who welcomed him warmly. Bharat's family had also seen better days, thanks to government schemes that had transformed the village.

"Do you know, Randhir?" Bharat said. "The government has provided us with housing, monthly financial support, medical facilities, and even 24/7 electricity and water. Life here is so comfortable now; no one wants to move to the city."

Randhir, however, noticed a lack of ambition in Bharat's words. "But what about your son's future? What are your plans for his development?" he asked. Bharat shrugged. "Why should I worry? The government takes care of everything."

That evening, back at his village home, Randhir shared his concerns with Jaya. "Am I doing the right thing, struggling in the city while others enjoy free benefits here?" Jaya, ever wise, responded, "Free lunches never last forever. We are on the right path, working hard for our children's future. They will grow up knowing the value of our efforts and will have the opportunities we never did."

Randhir slept peacefully that night, reassured by Jaya's words. The next morning, they boarded the train back to the city, ready to continue their journey of hard work and hope for a brighter future for their family..**PPA**

Story 14

Tragic tale of Joginder: Love, loss, and lingering conflict

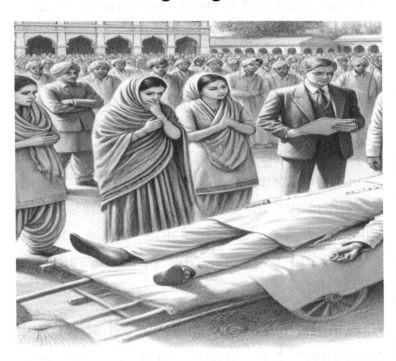

Joginder, a man in his mid-forties, had recently returned to India after spending two decades working tirelessly in the Middle East. He hailed from a small village in northern India and had left home at the age of 24 to join his maternal uncle in Saudi Arabia, working for an oil and gas company. His hard work earned him substantial remuneration, but after two decades abroad, he longed to return to his homeland. Upon his return, Joginder secured a job with a construction company, eager to settle into a new phase of life.

It was during the peak of the COVID-19 pandemic's second wave when Joginder joined the company. Fatalities were soaring, and the company was taking stringent measures to ensure worker safety, as manpower had already dwindled after a mass exodus during the first wave. Joginder, strong and vigilant, took all necessary precautions, but the virus was relentless.

One morning, Joginder woke up feeling heaviness in his chest and a sense of weakness. Initially, he dismissed it as fatigue from working at heights the previous night. However, as the symptoms worsened, suspicions of a COVID-19 infection arose. He was immediately quarantined and prescribed medication. On the seventh day, when most patients began showing improvement, Joginder's condition deteriorated rapidly. He was rushed to the largest multi-specialty hospital in the neighbouring town, but the situation there was grim.

The hospital was overcrowded, oxygen cylinders were being sold at exorbitant prices, and desperate families scrambled for resources. Joginder, despite the company's influence, was allotted a bed in the corridor. Life-saving antibiotics were administered, but the virus proved too strong. Joginder succumbed to the disease, leaving behind a legacy of hard work and a family shattered by grief.

The company's HR department immediately informed Joginder's family in the village. His wife, son, and five other relatives arrived at the hospital, guided by local labor union representatives who urged them to demand significant compensation from the company. As Joginder's body lay in the hospital corridor, his wife wept inconsolably while other family members, along with union leaders, negotiated with the company management.

The site in-charge, a respected figure, managed to strike a compensation deal. An advance of Rs. 2 lakhs was handed over for the cremation, with a commitment to resolve the remaining benefits once Joginder's elder son, Parminder, returned to the site after the cremation and final rites. The family left with Joginder's body, and the management sighed in relief at having resolved the immediate crisis.

Just as the management began enhancing safety measures to prevent further losses, a surprising development occurred. The next morning, the site security guard reported a group of 9-10 people, including a woman and two young girls, waiting at the gate to speak with the management.

When the site in-charge and HR manager met them, they were shocked to discover that the woman claimed to be Joginder's second wife. She presented Aadhaar cards, remittance records, and even a marriage photograph to substantiate her claim. The HR manager, taken aback, informed the assistant compensation commissioner and insisted that the two families resolve their dispute legally before any further payments could be made.

Ravikant, the union leader, escalated the matter, demanding immediate compensation. He threatened a complete work stoppage, prompting the HR manager to seek police intervention. A posse was deployed to prevent unrest, and messages were sent to Joginder's village to summon his first wife and son.

The situation worsened as the laborers, incited by union leaders, resorted to damaging construction equipment. A police lathi charge ensued, leaving several laborers injured. Amidst the chaos, Joginder's first family arrived at the site. The local MLA, Rashid Khan, a pragmatic and respected leader, intervened to mediate the dispute. He addressed the crowd, urging them to maintain peace and assured them of justice.

The two families, however, failed to reach an agreement. Joginder's first wife was adamant about retaining 75% of the compensation, while the second wife demanded an equal share to support her young daughters. Ravikant's attempts to mediate also proved futile. The management insisted that the families resolve their differences before approaching the compensation commissioner.

Four years have passed, and the conflict remains unresolved. A third claimant has now surfaced, alleging to be another dependent of Joginder from his previous workplace. With only one year left before the compensation amount is forfeited and deposited to government funds as unclaimed, the families continue to suffer. Instigated by people with no stakes in their plight, the stalemate endures.

The tragedy of Joginder's life extends beyond his untimely death. His legacy, once rooted in hard work and sacrifice, is now mired in discord and uncertainty—a stark reminder of the complexities of human relationships and the impact of unresolved conflicts..**PPA**

Story 15

The gang of Dhansar: Friendship and life

This year, the batch of Class 10th was notoriously unruly, to the extent that the new principal, Mr. Robin, who had taken over a year ago, was heard saying in the teacher's room, "I don't understand how to deal with Class X. It gives me a desperate feeling that they're playing the tune, and I'm dancing to it. A few of the students are really bright, but I'm concerned about the school's reputation, which has for decades boasted of at least a dozen students securing 90% and above in the board examinations."

Mr. Francis, who was close to the boys, listened with a sigh of defiance. He was comfortable with the maverick behavior of young boys, which he believed bred comprehensive development in children. True to his belief, in the pre-board examinations, the batch broke the school record as fifteen students crossed the 90% mark. The surprise inclusion was Shambhu, the bully of the batch, who had exemplary debating skills and a strong command of language, though he barely studied for 20 days before the board exams.

Disaster struck on the day the board results were declared. The students of Class 10th rushed to school to check their results, only to find that the batch had fared unexpectedly poorly, with 17 failures and only one student, the brightest, Rajesh, securing 80%. A few students cried like small children, while others lay on the grass, distraught and awe-struck. Shambhu, one of the sixteen first-divisioners, immediately got into his act. "This is sheer conspiracy by Principal Mr. Robin, who never liked our batch," he declared. A few of his close cronies agreed and planned a protest against the principal, but they were dissuaded by Rajesh's sane counsel. "But where will we get admission with such poor marks?" cried Bhatt. Parents, hearing the outcome, rushed to the school to pick up their boys.

While active discussions were underway in every home about the future course of action, news spread that Shambhu and ten of his batchmates had decided to go to Devigarh to explore admission opportunities. A few boys traveled to Devigarh and were struck with excitement upon reaching the city, renowned for its development and modernity. They rushed to the government college and discovered that most of them could secure admission. They sent word through a friend, who didn't find the place academically appealing and returned home. Soon, twenty boys from the same batch congregated in Devigarh. A few who missed the threshold marks were also admitted, thanks to the persuasion of Shambhu and Sanjay, a short boy blessed with grandfatherly wisdom. Finally, the boys' worries dissipated, and their tumultuous journey began.

The hostel rooms were reasonably well-furnished, and the mess served a truly exotic spread of food. Sanjay and two others decided to stay outside the hostel for a freer, more unobtrusive life. Smoking and occasional drinking had already become part of their pastime indulgences, and soon their room on the top floor became a den for intruders from the coalfield town of Dhansaar, now in

Jharkhand. Winter had set in, and they discovered that the first snowfall had occurred at Himpath. Having seen coal dust all their lives, the idea of experiencing snowfall was too alluring to resist. Ten of them decided to board the slow train from Kalki to Himpath. They packed into a small train compartment and locked the door from all sides. Soon, other travelers with reservations started knocking, but the boys refused to budge.

The ticket collector arrived with the railway protection team, and the boys, realizing the folly of being ticketless travelers, panicked. Vinod suggested they jump off the train from the valley side of the bogey to avoid arrest and parental repercussions. Without seeing anything, they jumped, sliding down bushes for quite a distance. Once they landed in the plains, they ran until they felt safe. However, their desire to see the snowfall was so intense that they regrouped, bought tickets, and boarded the same train again.

Himpath was covered in snow. Vinod exclaimed, "I feel like I've become colorblind; all I can see is black and white!" They found a lodge and took two rooms. When the waiter asked if they needed anything "hot," Pillai, a simple teenager, responded, "Just warm dal and roti for ten," and shut the door. Exhausted, the boys fell asleep under the scanty quilts provided. The next morning, they were reluctant to leave the warmth of their quilts despite the waiter's calls. Adjusting to the cold climate was a challenge for boys from the warm coalfield region.

Over the next few days, they roamed all the prominent places like Mall Road, the skating rink, and local gardens, clicking numerous photographs. Debu, one of the naughtiest, suggested exploring the lower road, rumored to be exciting. A few ventured out and returned with stories that became part of their growing lore.

Back in Devigarh, students returning from other places shared their tales. The boys spent the next few days reminiscing over scintillating stories laced with facts and fiction, indulging in booze, smoking, and card games. Life was fun, away from the watchful eyes of parents.

However, the first semester exams were disastrous for the boys from Dhansaar. Furious parents wrote letters filled with warnings and expectations, urging them to focus on their studies. This wake-up call brought most of them back on track. Shambhu made it to the college hockey team, while Vinod was praised for his artistic skills. Sanjay was elected Joint Secretary of the Student Union and became a troubleshooter for all coalfield boys.

After two years, they completed their intermediate examinations and went their separate ways. Life scattered them across different paths, each facing their own trials and tribulations.

Two decades later, social media reconnected the gang. Soon, fifteen members formed a WhatsApp group, which became a lively medium of engagement. They decided to meet in the capital city, with Sanjay organizing the event at his sprawling farmhouse. It was a two-day get-together attended by all members. They reminisced, laughed, and behaved like childhood friends. The families bonded, and the group now meets annually, counting down the days to their next reunion..**PPA**

Author

Prem Prakash Akhauri is a seasoned Human Resources (HR) Consultant with extensive experience leading HR functions in esteemed public and private sector organizations. His professional journey and accolades are showcased on LinkedIn. Beyond his expertise in HR, he is a prolific writer and accomplished author.

His debut e-book, *"Khayal...Mere Apne!"*, resonated deeply with readers, celebrated for its simplicity and its insightful exploration of human behavior, thoughts, and emotions. Building on its success, he penned two more captivating compilations, *"Abhivyakti...Khayalo ki Ravani"* and *"Dhun...Khayalo ki Gungunahat"*, all available on **Pothi.com** and **Amazon Kindle**. These works reflect his unique ability to weave profound ideas into relatable expressions.

For years, Prem Prakash Akhauri has been documenting his reflections, feelings, and life experiences through his writings. He encourages introspective minds to articulate their thoughts—not merely as a pursuit of self-contentment or tranquility but as a significant contribution to the creative domain.

He firmly believes that expressing thoughts in words is not only an art but also a deeply fulfilling journey for the soul.

Acknowledgment

I would like to extend my gratitude to Seema Akhauri for her meticulous proofreading of my book. Her keen eye for detail and dedication to refining words have been invaluable in bringing this work to life. Thank you for ensuring clarity and precision throughout the book.

Images: AI generated

Disclaimer:

This collection of short stories is a work of fiction. All characters, events, and places depicted in these stories are purely the product of the author's imagination. Any resemblance to actual persons, living or deceased, or to any real-life events, places, or institutions is purely coincidental and unintended. The stories are crafted solely for entertainment and creative expression.

Request:

In due course of time, the author may consider weaving the short stories into a story book.Kindly refrain from reproducing the storyline.

Thank you

Made in United States
Troutdale, OR
01/22/2025